Flip the Switch

By Michelle Jeffalone

Change your life to a
Positive & Joyful existence
through Mindfulness.

www.MchelleJeffalone.com

www.michellejeffalone.com

Ordering Information:
Quantity sales. Special discounts are available on quantity purchases by corporations, associations, and others. For details, contact the publisher at the address above.

Printed in the United States of America

Flip the Switch : Change your life to a positive & joyful existence through mindfulness / Michelle Jeffalone
ISBN-13: 978-1546375715
ISBN-10: 1546375716
1 Self Help. 2. Fiction

First Edition

PREFACE

In the past I believed that I was not supposed to be joyful all of the time, that there were only moments of joy and that there had to be a reason or experience causing this happiness... Let me tell you my friends, it's powerful to have all of the good feelings inside bubble up to the surface and achieve a joyful & positive existence.

In this book, you can count on me to reinforce good habits, share wisdom through stories, and support you with tangible skills which are summarized as key takeaways at the end of each chapter well organized actionable results. You may also view this as a mindfulness practice; being present with ourselves to acknowledge our actions and thought patterns, breaking them down to our internal and external beliefs & harmonizing them with our emotions, which are derived from our thoughts.

We'll embrace existentialism; there is an emphasis on the existence of you as an individual person, as a free and responsible agent determining your own development through acts of free will in harmony with your thought patterns, internal and external beliefs & emotions, which are derived from your thoughts. Flip the Switch wraps up with a practical strategy to build a community of like-minded people. It is my hope to reach others on a metaphorical cliff, ready to take the leap... creating and living into a new mindset for the betterment of their life.

Honestly, Chapter 4 "Wholeness" was challenging for me in a way that I didn't expect. I had worked diligently for years to better myself, invested my time and attention to all the familiar inroads that may sound familiar to you: I spoke with friends on a similar path, read self-help books, watched YouTube videos for so called "enlightenment", attended workshops and even sought out learning through observations of others. I was happy, even joyful and in a positive mindset. There were so many years when I wasn't in this state of being that it sometimes overrode the grey matter in my brain to make me believe there was still a struggle, still a fight to become this thing I already was, a joyful person with a positive mindset.

Thank you to my loving family, friends, teachers in this life, mentors and contemporaries who taught, supported, encouraged and nudged me along the way; I am truly grateful and blessed with a loving and supportive community. Thank you God, I am grateful.

SPECIAL NOTE TO
THE READER

This book is not intended as a substitute for the good advice of physicians. It is suggested that the reader seek the expertise of a trained physician or enlightened health-care practitioner for diagnosis, treatment, and guidance in respect to any symptoms that may require diagnosis or medical attention.

To protect the privacy of certain individuals, the names and identifying details have been changed.

Also, for the general reader, and especially for those readers who do not have experience with meditation or mindfulness, it is suggested that the "Key Learning" at the end of each chapter be read first, and then the chapter should be read from beginning to end. It has been found that this method works best in making sense of certain complex information and also grounds the key insights necessary to understanding further chapters. Also, it is recommended that the chapters of the book be read in sequential order, as each chapter builds on the information developed in the preceding chapter.

Michelle Jeffalone, MBA

CONTENTS

Chapter 1. PEACEFULNESS
Calm your mind and thoughts with compassion

Transform your life by making one simple decision, to be positive and joyful. Creating the space for new habits to take root in your mind is obtainable through freeing oneself from an overwhelmed state of mind. In chapter 1 we will discuss owning our decisions, implementing compassion into our emotional processes, reframing the situation and move on with the emotion you decide to fill your head with.

One way to feel empowered is to slow things down, i.e. your thoughts. Slowing your thoughts during the day and welcoming a calm presence in your life begins by creating quiet time for yourself. I suggest doing this preemptively before or after a stressful task in order to reset yourself to a more peaceful mindset. Creating a moments of quiet space allows us to recalibrate and slow our thoughts down. It all begins with the belief that you are able to have an intelligent, yet calm, thought process instead of racing, stressful thoughts keeping us awake or occupying our valuable time during the day.

Creating this quiet time and becoming present in the moment is a way of reconnecting with our calm nature, and it feels good. Breath work is a way to be present. Simply noticing your breath and then counting your breaths for 30 seconds can have a positive impact on your mindset and calming your presence. I suggest you set a timer so you will not think about how much time you have left while doing this exercise. In chapter 5 we'll review a more advanced breath technique within a compassionate mindfulness exercise but for now try counting your breath for 30 seconds.

- Sit comfortably or lie down
- Set a timer for 30 seconds
- Breathe normal steady breathes, counting each inhale and exhale

We've all had sleepless nights with thoughts racing through our minds. We have the ability to slow and eventually let go of them. When I have had racing thoughts at night, I found writing a list of tasks is helpful to slow things down in my mind. You needn't worry about the order of the items. It is simply important to get the list out of our thought process by putting it on paper. Then, I reframe how I view my mind having racing thoughts. I think of the process with compassion and gratitude. My mind is so considerate, that it will remind me repeatedly of the tasks I need to complete the next day. How organized and loving of it. I imagine sending my mind love from my heart and this seems to quell its need to remind me. Somehow deep down I know everything is under control and my mind can take a break until the morning, trusting that I will remember to look at the list in the morning.

Entrust in your minds ability to let go of the list while you rest. This has the effect of slowing down your thoughts which allows for a restful night's sleep. I have found it useful before my head hits my pillow to say out loud with kindness to myself, "I'm tired and I'm going to sleep, I will sleep the whole night through and wake up feeling rested and joyful". It's another layer of granting permission for my entire being to relax and sleep deeply.

Be compassionate with your mind and its racing thoughts at night:
- Write down tasks
- Be grateful to your mind for staying on the ball and even send it love
- Give permission to your mind to relax
- Allow a sense of calm to overcome you
- State aloud your intentions to sleep restfully

"I'm tired and I'm going to sleep, I will sleep the whole night through and wake up feeling rested and joyful".

If you're feeling overwhelmed in waking hours, do the next thing that make sense and do it mindfully; that's what I do!

I am at my best the first 4 days after a truly relaxing vacation. You know the feeling, when there isn't anything in the world worth stressing out over. When our minds are still in vacation mode, we believe the work we have to do will get done, one step at a time. It is important to note that we have the ability to implement the same tranquil state of mind in our lives at any given moment, even if a vacation is months away. One technique to accomplish this is the use of visualizations. Imagine you have an invisible calming helmet. You can go so far as to imagine that when you put this helmet on, it holds a scene where you are on a boat sailing in the ocean or on a beach. I personally use a helmet filled with calm space. When I have too many thoughts in my mind, I superimpose a calm frame of mind over my head. Seriously, imagine you take off the helmet that has all the kaleidoscope of thoughts whirling around and replace it with the visualization of a tranquil tropical ocean. It's a better view.

Slow things down, invoke calm thoughts in your life

- o Remove the invisible helmet with a kaleidoscope of thoughts swirling around
- o Put on the invisible helmet with a tropical scene that is calming

Now that you have a calming visual and slowed your thoughts down, you do the next thing that makes sense, and do it mindfully. Make a list for yourself for the day and prioritize it. Choose the one item that makes sense to do and complete it. In this moment, be mindful of the steps you need to take to accomplish the task fully. As you work on each step be fully present and enjoy yourself. Allow other thoughts to enter your mind and float away like a cloud. Allow yourself to let go of the emotions and judgment of the thoughts which occur in your mind. Two ways I've found that allow my mind to relax are to either trust myself to remember valuable thoughts at a later time or write thoughts down and then let go of trying to remember them. If you're able, think of those thoughts as separate from the work we're doing in the moment and enjoying. Accomplish this one task completely and mindfully before moving to the next task on your list. I celebrate the completion of tasks by checking them off. There's nothing better at the end of the day than a list of check marks next to my to do list.

Do the next thing that makes sense and do it mindfully

- o Make a list of tasks and prioritize it
- o Choose a task that makes sense to do first
- o Find enjoyment while completing it, smile & engage your heart

It's your life and your mind. You make the decision to change the pace of the racing thoughts to a slower calm existence in this life. When I'm stressed out I can't think clearly, I'm not in touch with my heart and somehow I feel separated. Stay connected to yourself, notice what's going on in your body when you're feeling overwhelmed. Where do you feel it? Is it the same muscles that tense up every time you feel stressed out? Being aware is the first step towards a calm, peace and joy.

Becoming aware helps you own your decisions; owning your current mindset is crucial to giving yourself permission to feel joyful. This may require a shift to your current state of mind. For example, own your choice to feel jittery or nervous. Embrace fully how your body feels in this moment, then send your tense muscles compassion. Usually when I'm stressed out, my shoulders rise up to meet my ears; once I realize this is happening I intentionally squeeze them up higher and create more tension in my body, then I consciously release it, take a breath, sink into my heart space and send my body compassion. My body thinks it's protecting me from something stressful. Get to know your body's cues for when it perceives a stressful or threatening situation arising – the situational triggers (we'll discuss triggers more in Chapter 2). This practice enables you to be more aware when the tension is arising in your body, then send that area love and compassion, acknowledging your mind's protective nature and being thankful for it. The simple exercise of acknowledging my body's reaction to protect me, and sending it compassion, allows me to feel a fuller sense of relaxation once I release the exaggerated tension. I repeat tensing my body muscles and releasing with compassion repeatedly, then make the conscious choice to stay in a relaxed physical state. Once we have the muscle memory of what 'relaxed' feels like in our body and mind, it becomes easier to slide into that state when we become aware of a nervousness coming from within. Move forward through your choice to leave behind nervousness, and embrace a calm, positive mental and physical space. It's in our nature to be joyful. Own this decision and reset your psyche once you notice you've wandered off course to the Netherlands of tension.

Move forward through the choice to change your mindset

- Embrace fully how your body feels in this moment
- Send your tense muscles compassion
- Find the tension in parts of your body
- Add tension those areas or your whole body
- Relax and release it
- Take a breath, smile, sink into your heart & feel yourself in a relaxed state
- Notice the next time you feel tension and shift to a more peaceful mindset

Own the thoughts and emotions we allow ourselves to embody with compassion. Once we own that it has been our decision to think and feel a certain way, for example, sorrowful, there may be some piggy backing feelings attached of guilt or shame. How could I have felt this way for so long, did I enjoy it? Remember the compassion piece; be kind to YOURSELF when YOU have these self-reflective Ah-Ha moments. When I became aware that I was giving myself permission to wallow over my first real heartache, I realized I had an attachment to the feeling of sorrow. I felt guilty for finding some sort of fulfillment in wallowing in this feeling. My deep truth was that I had embraced it and believed that it defined me. Feeling sadness had somehow justified the relationship's existence, such that I had experienced real love because I was now really sad; a proclamation to the world that I had been in love. The deep connection I had to self-validating my former relationship was powerful, and I became riddled with guilt and embarrassment. How could I have worn this badge of sorrow so flagrantly? What was I trying to prove when I exposed the world to my grief? The world I want to live in is a joyful one and I knew I had to embrace my emotions differently, to let go of the attachment to wallowing...

Once I realized I'd been wallowing, I gave myself the gift of compassion. Of course I was hurt that the relationship was over. It can be sad when things end, even when it is our decision to end them. I tend to dance to really loud music on my headset when these moments arise. I'm not able to feel anything but joyful when I'm dancing. Once in a positive mind frame, I smiled and asked myself the difficult questions. Why did I believe it was necessary to feel sorrow still? What made me feel honorable in holding into this grief? Did I have something to prove to myself or others? I was proving something to myself by extending the sorrow. I had loved deeply and believed it was honorable to extend my grief to the depth I had loved this man. In the end, I didn't find value in holding onto the sorrow. I had been honorable in loving deeply while in the relationship. Now that it was over, I chose to honor myself by moving on and creating space for a positive and joyful existence - which is my true nature. By embracing my personal choice to feel and present myself authentically, I found empowerment. In that Ah—Ha moment, I changed my mindset, by following these simple steps.

Own your decision to feel a certain way & flip the switch to a joyful existence:

- Compassionately acknowledge that you've embraced an emotion or thought process
- Fill your personal space with joyful body expressions (like smiling) and thoughts that make you feel good
- Find the root cause or belief of why you're embracing an emotion (like sadness) and wallowing
- Rethink its rationality
- Reframe the situation that caused your decision to feel a certain way and make it positive, move on with the emotion you choose to fill your head space with

Key Learning

Use breath work to calm your mind from racing thoughts and enable peace to enter

- Count the breathes you take in and out for 30 seconds
- Sit comfortably or lie down
- Set a timer for 30 seconds

- Breathe normal steady breathes, counting each inhale & exhale

Free oneself from an overwhelmed state of mind
- Be compassionate with your mind and its racing thoughts
- Write down tasks
- Be grateful to your mind for staying on the ball and even send it love
- Give permission to your mind to relax
- Allow a sense of calm to overcome you

State aloud your intentions to sleep restfully:

"I'm tired and I'm going to sleep,

I will sleep the whole night through and wake up feeling rested and joyful"

Slow things down.
- Invoke calm thoughts in your life
- Remove the invisible helmet with a kaleidoscope of thoughts swirling around
- Put on the invisible helmet with a tropical scene that is calming

Do the next thing that makes sense and do it mindfully

- Make a list of tasks and prioritize it
- Choose a task that makes sense to do first
- Find enjoyment while completing it, smile & engage your heart

Move forward through the choice to change your mindset

- Embrace fully how your body feels in this moment
- Send your tense muscles compassion
- Find the tension in parts of your body
- Add tension those areas or your whole body
- Relax and release it
- Take a breath, smile, sink into your heart & feel yourself in a relaxed state
- Notice the next time you feel tension and shift to a more peaceful mindset

Own your decision to feel a certain way & flip the switch to a joyful existence:

- Compassionately acknowledge that you've embraced an emotion or thought process
- Fill your personal space with joyful body expressions (like smiling) and thoughts that make you feel good
- Find the root cause or belief of why you're embracing an emotion (like sadness) and wallowing

- Rethink its rationality
- Reframe the situation that caused your decision to feel a certain way
- And make it positive, move on with the emotion you choose to fill your head space with.

Chapter 2: CHOOSE EMPOWERMENT

Declare a positive and joyful existence

On the path to consciously deciding to be happy and fulfilled... there's work to do; maintaining a joyful presence is a mindful practice of compassionately reminding ourselves that we are already happy. I use the mantra "I am naturally joyful". We all backslide from time to time into a negative state of mind. It may be useful to find a phrase to engrain the thought of flipping the switch to joy, while in the process of resetting our mindset. Another phrase I learned from one of Britain's top healers and motivational speakers, Marisa Peer is "I am enough". Years ago she called me on stage to discuss love, it was a moving exercise we did together where she helped me walk through self-love and feeling it in abundance. Acknowledging that I am enough was a profound lesson in my personal evolution. I started off repeating "I am naturally joyful" and then moved into using the phrase, "I am enough". Both serve a purpose, I found the latter more all-encompassing of myself because I'm not always feeling joyful and being enough moves me to a peaceful state of mind. There is no right or wrong, if a phrase feels good to you, use it. It's powerful to repeat a mantra to yourself before spending time with colleagues who haven't made the choice to be joyful and positive in their thoughts and speech. Let's face it, not everyone is on the same path and this can be frustrating. Remember that what you do, is your choice. Being positive and joyful is a choice. Embrace the decision, live into it, and give it away for free, even when we feel surrounded by negative energy suckers!

Empower yourself and declare positivity and a joyful existence. After all, it's in your nature. If this resonates with you then you're off to a good start. It took me years to realize this truth for myself. Although I seemed optimistic from the outside, I wasn't truly sold on the idea of an inner joyful presence. I've had a series of what I'd call hobby businesses over the course of my life. In my 20's they were fashion based, and later I expressed my entrepreneurial spirit through performance art. These creative outlets brought joy into my world; I was able to leave my boring life and let in moments of happiness. The truth I came to realize is that I am an individual person acting as a free and responsible agent determining my own development through acts of my free will. Existentialism at its finest! I was holding onto the belief that those acts of creativity were the moments I would feel joy. This wasn't enough any longer. I didn't want sparse moments of joy; I was ready for the full Monty… a different existence. This was the moment I changed my belief system or my story; my truth is that deep down inside it's in my nature to be joyful and positive. I had held onto an archaic belief that in life I was not supposed to be happy all of the time, that there were only moments of joy and there has to be a reason or experience causing this happiness. Let me tell you my friends, it's powerful to have all of the good feelings inside bubble up to the surface and really bring forward the best version of ourselves that we can achieve. Then our ideas and self-determined success factors can be realized in a meaningful way. It's a lot of fun.

It's my hope to reach individuals with the quest of becoming their 'best selves', maybe even share a bit of knowledge or new wording of knowledge. The language we use is powerful. And at the same time, it's one of my fundamental beliefs that we are our own best guru.

At this point in our journey, I challenge you to answer the following questions:

- ○ What's been your major learning, insight, or discovery so far in your journey to a joyful existence?

o   If there was one thing that hasn't yet been said in general, or that we (as the reader) haven't said to ourselves in order to reach a deeper level of understanding and clarity? What would you say to yourself right now?

The achievement of not only creating a positive inner self, but also creating a positive life, is one of my favorite litmus tests. How positive is the life surrounding you?

How positive are the friends you interact with? We've talked about how we choose our own thought process, which creates our true nature of being positive and joyful, but one aspect we haven't spoken about yet is how we perceive the world and the people around us. One of my greatest learning's was allowing myself to hear what others would say to me – in a positive tone. Once I put the belief into practice that the people around me were being authentically positive, it acted as a crutch to enable me to respond similarly. After all, like attracts like. I use the word 'crutch', which to some may imply weakness, but I think of it more as a compassionate leaning tool to get me over the hump. I was vulnerable in the beginning of my transformation to a positive mindset, sometimes I would backslide into my old thought patterns and more negative reactions. We will all have moments of backsliding, don't beat yourself up too much. Instead, send yourself compassion and reset yourself. I would say 'What a good memory I have of past experiences with this person. It is now safe to let go and live in the present moment'. In other words, I acknowledge and honor my memory of this person and I lovingly embraced the idea that he/she is coming from a positive light in the present, which allows me the space to live into my true nature and respond positively.

When those negative energy sucker buggers are around us, how we choose to hear them and their message is powerful. It's a direct reflection of our inner mind. Let's say that you're with someone who gossips about others. We can choose to reframe this person's intentions; they need to vent in a harmless way. Once we reframe their habit in a positive light, there is no trigger for us to buy into, it's no longer a negative interaction. Our brains are naturally sensitive to negativity and ready to spring into action to defend us, but it cannot distinguish between a real threat and our grumpy gossiping co-worker. The primitive protection response part of our brains turns a good amount of its attention to the negative source and your happy mood is shot. Let's say you were a cave person and you heard a rustle in the bushes. It would be in your best interest if the fight or flight instinct kicked in and you fled the area. We no longer live in that era, but our brains are hardwired to go towards the negative in protection mode. How loving our mind is, how wonderful of it to try and keep us safe in this way. It's up to us to override these prehistoric reactions we're hardwired with.

We may begin this journey of growth and mental maturity by reframing the situation. When we reframe the intentions by asking ourselves "How can I see this gossiping person differently?" we are able to free our minds from holding onto and buying into the other person's behavior, then they will have little or no effect on us. In the transformative stages of embracing others good intentions, it was challenging to flip the switch to positivity, especially once I allowed myself to be triggered. I had a backup plan, in these moments I would speak frankly with others stating that "I'm uncomfortable hearing you talk about others that way and it doesn't feel good participating. Can we talk about something else?" Engaging people in this way provided self-preservation of my positive and joyful mindset while alleviating my brain of negativity. I was no longer engaging with my own trigger towards negative emotions. Sometimes I needed to take initiative and change the situation I was exposing myself to for my own self maintenance.

By hearing others from a positive light, it allows us the space to mirror them and respond accordingly. Mirroring is a well-documented natural occurrence for human beings. We have a natural tendency to mimic people's body language and tone in a conversation. Many use this technique to bond with others. People feel more comfortable because we are seen as more alike when we look and talk like one another.

When we take on self-leadership while in a conversation by listening to and responding in a positive light to others, we pave the way for others to move in this direction as well. Mirroring is a helpful trick when at the office with others who, for whatever reason, are not in the same mindset. Start by mirroring their body language and move to a more open, joyful, relaxed power position. They just may follow your lead!

Another technique to maintain a positive outlook when dealing with difficult people is what I call the 90/10 rule. You add a positive word for the 90 percent good in the person and leave the 10 percent grumpiness in play. Maybe I can't wrap my head around that the gossiping colleague is 100 percent coming from a positive place, so I give them 90 percent positivity and 10 percent grumpy. I think of one word that creates a feeling of joy or peace from within myself and associate it with that person; compassionate, peaceful, content, grateful, abundance and acceptance are some of my favorites. Using these 90/10 words transforms our interactions to be in line with the emotion the word creates within us. Your brain doesn't know the difference between what you imagine to be true and reality.

Once I had a roommate who was dead set on the belief that there was always a problem in the kitchen. Whether it was the dishes weren't put away correctly, someone was using their spices, the dishwasher was run when it wasn't full, or it was someone else's turn to clean; she always brought up an issue in the kitchen. After some time, I came to realize there wasn't a problem. It was another Ah-Hah moment. I simply stopped believing there were problems in the kitchen. This shift allowed me to see her in the 90/10 light. She complained a lot so I gave her the 10 percent grump award and I also gave her the 90 percent positivity. I chose to think of the word peaceful when interacting with her about the kitchen. I embraced the feeling I had when thinking of the word peaceful and superimposed it on her, believing she was 90 percent peaceful. My mindset was: there isn't a problem & you're 90% peaceful. You know, it worked. Frankly my reactions to her shifted to a peaceful mode and somehow to my surprise - she became more peaceful in the process. Admittedly, she remained 10% grumpy while we lived together, but it no longer had an effect on my responses or me.

I saw her as a peaceful person and responded to her from that same space. My life became more joyful when dealing with a difficult person by thinking of a word that evoked a positive emotion in me, then I would react and respond from a positive mental space.

90/10 switching from 100% jerk

- Compassionately imagine the person has characteristics
- or values you positively identify with
- Create a story around the person that allows you to find a reason to like them
- Envision the story before or during interactions with them to shift your thoughts about them to a more positive light

OR

- Find a word that brings about compassion for the person who is difficult to deal with
- Use the word as a mantra when interacting with them to shift your thinking about them to the positive

If it's not possible to hear and reframe people speaking to a more positive light, or add a 90/10 word to your thoughts when speaking with them, then approach the situation with self-preservation in mind. Ultimately, compassionately listening to people and holding a deep belief within ourselves that people are innately good and positive then flips the switch from choosing empowerment, to 'being' empowered, joyful and positive by nature.

Own it! You've earned it! It's in our nature to be positive and joyful, embrace and own it as our true character. Honestly, this step was challenging for me in a way that I didn't expect. I had worked diligently for years to better myself, invested my time and attention to all the familiar inroads that may sound familiar to you: I spoke with friends on a similar path, read self-help books, watched YouTube videos for so called "enlightenment", attended workshops and even sought out learning through observations of others. I was happy, even joyful and in a positive mindset. There were so many years when I wasn't in this state of mind that it sometimes overrode the grey matter in my brain to make me believe there was still a struggle, still a fight to become this thing I already was. It was then I realized that I was in the routine of working towards being happy. It was unfathomable that I had achieved my goal. I kicked the habit! I decided to give up the underlying hook, the longing to work towards success in the future, and began to embrace compassionately who I was in that moment, a joyful person with a positive mindset.

The next challenge I faced was externally, with my loved ones. You may find yourself hanging in the balance with friends and family, tittering on the cusp of their previous beliefs of you, and having to transition those you love towards buying into this person you've become.

In the context of reframing who you've become to loved ones, helping them see you differently, I took the direct approach. People get used to patterns of behavior and believe it or not, it takes up to 9 interactions to recreate their image of you. For example, when in conversations with my loved ones, they expected the same old response I use to give, which was not in line with my positive nature. I was initially hurt that they didn't seem to notice how I had transformed in thought and deed. I then realized I had been unaware of the impact I had on my environment as an individual. Then accountability kicked in. I was responsible for my actions and reactions which incurred a type of projection people believed of me, and elicited a specific response from my closest of loved ones. My internal world effected my external world, I had projected my sometimes negative attitude into the world and it got used to responding a certain way to what I was emoting . Fill in the blank of how we've emoted in the past: with negativity, lonely, sadness, desperation, scarcity, shame, guilt, pessimism, jealousy, etc.

Reframing yourself to your loved ones:

- o Be open and share your internal process of change and growth with the external world
- o Vocally share a reframing of yourself when you feel labeled with the 'old you' by others
- o Honor the person you were and the person you've become with compassion
- o Have compassion for the people around you, changing how you're seen externally takes time

My direct approach was to openly share the changes I was intentionally making in my life to bring them on board during the process, and if it had the added bonus of pulling them along in their path of growth, all the better. It's not wise to have this loaded expectation when sharing your journey, it may cause resentment from your loved ones and interpreted that you don't think they're good enough just as they are.

Everyone is on their own journey and the best way to lead sometimes, is to model the material. Once I had shared the new baseline for my behavior of positivity and joy, it was much easier to have discussions when I felt put into a box of my old behaviors. I could say compassionately "I'm on a different path now. That's not my thought process. I no longer buy into the emotions that used to fuel my decisions, now I see it this way…". Acknowledge where you've been with compassion for yourself, remove any associated guilt or shame, and state your present mindset.

Key Learning

Backsliding Strategies

Make a conscious decision to be joyful and positive, it's in your nature

- Flip the switch to positive when you backslide
- Check in with yourself
- Allow yourself to hear what others say to you in a positive tone and respond accordingly
- Initiate mirroring positive body language and facial expressions
- Own it you've earned it, allow yourself to believe you're positive and joyful

90/10 rule; create a story or word for a difficult person which enables you to have positive thoughts about them while interacting together

- Compassionately imagine the person has characteristics or values you positively identify with
- Create a story around the person that allows you to find a reason to like them

- o Envision the story before or during interactions with them to shift your thoughts about them to a more positive light

OR

- o Find a word that brings about compassion for the person who is difficult to deal with
- o Use the word as a mantra when interacting with them to shift your thinking about them to the positive

Reframe yourself to others with compassion

- o Reframing yourself to your loved ones:
- o Be open and share your internal process of change and growth with the external world
- o Vocally share a reframing of yourself when you feel labeled with the 'old you' by others
- o Acknowledge where you've been with compassion for yourself, remove any associated guilt or shame
- o State your present mindset to loved ones
- o Have compassion for the people around you, changing how you're seen externally takes time

Chapter 3. *BE MASTERFUL IN WRITING YOUR STORY*
Choose language mindfully

The language we use internally, in our thoughts, and in external dialog has a powerful impact on our existence. How we cognitively frame, create a personal story, or give meaning to our lives can actually have a real effect on us at a genetic level. Epigenetics suggest that we are a product of interfacing with our environment, what we experience in our lives may affect our genetics. Positive thinking enhances our well-being at a cellular level, which is backed by research.

Our brain doesn't know the difference between our imagination and reality. The more we fill our minds with positive thinking coupled with action, the more we will live in a consistent, joyful existence. Live into the words you use to describe yourself. In chapter 1 we discussed owning our decisions, implementing compassion into our emotional processes, reframing the situation and move on with the emotion you decide to fill your head with. This next skill is a derivative of that methodology. We're honing in on being mindful of the language we use internally. The idle mind chatter that so often we're not aware even exists.

As an avid jogger, I go jogging for exercise and because I love doing it! There was a time when I would dread going jogging, even if I enjoyed the process once I was outside moving my body in the rhythm that's uniquely mine. I thought to myself that I had to "get in shape". I beat myself up when I didn't go for a run as planned, throwing in negative self-talk that I was lazy and deserved to be lumpy around the edges. This resulted in me feeling guilty, unfit and unhealthy... gaining weight with every breath. Okay, that's a little bit of an exaggeration, but I did feel like I was gaining weight because I didn't go!

The negative spiral had me in its grips. I was living out the effects of the words I used internally to my external world. I then would give up and eat my favorite indulgence food - French fries at lunch, thinking 'it doesn't matter, I've already missed working out, I'm unfit and gaining weight by the minute, I give up". Maybe you can relate? I cannot tell you how empowering it was when I flipped the switch on this scenario. I became mindful of the self-chatter I had recorded in my mind when I missed a workout and created a new recording, sending compassion and kindness to myself (see chapter 1). And secondly, I flipped the language I used, the internal dialog.

I began to fully enjoying myself when I had French fries, and I still do, I reveled in the deliciousness of them enjoying each bite dipped in mayonnaise and ketchup. This one food became a wonderful indulgence that I love and am not giving up. That's not saying I eat them every day, but there have been odd weeks where I've had them 3 or 4 times! When I thought about working out I decided I was 'staying fit' not 'getting fit'. When I missed a workout I would fully participate in whatever I chose to do in its place. I acknowledge that jogging is a part of my life long term, it has been and will be. If I miss a day, I will go tomorrow, providing the compassion for myself that I don't always get to go jogging and yes, it's disappointing to not get to do the thing that makes me feel so good physically and emotionally. I acknowledge the feeling of sadness attached to the disappointment and then let it go. I then filled my mind with a joyful thought about the task I decided to do instead of working out. *It is key to feel how you feel in that moment, release it and then fill that space with an enjoyable emotion of your choice. This is another time when stating a mantra like "I am enough" (from Chapter 2) may be helpful so that negative emotions and thoughts like shame or guilt aren't able to stay attach while you're releasing the emotions surrounding not working out.

A scenario might be that I have to work late on a project and will miss my chance to go jogging. I feel sad about not going jogging, let it go and remind myself that I am at peace knowing I'll finish a project. I began to work out more regularly once I thought in positive a tone about the events surrounding it, missing it once in a while, and eating carb laden foods in order to replace the endorphin boost with a serotonin supplement. I began forgiving myself and became mindful of how I spoke to myself.

It's empowering to live into the words that we use to describe ourselves, and delete those myths which devalue our natural loving self. I thought of myself as an occasional jogger with spurts of getting fit, but I had been jogging for over 15 years! It was time to delete this story and start telling myself that I am a jogger, have been for most of my life, and will be for as long as I'm able. Staying fit is a part of my self-loving naturally. Another myth was that "I was not good enough" for x, y, z …. you fill in the blank here: success, a loving relationship, to be happy. It's a myth most of us live with in our lives and it takes away from our true nature to be positive and joyful. Staying mindful that our declaration to be joyful and positive means keeping it real with ourselves and owning the myths that are destructive.

Ask yourself questions as you look at an area where you feel you're not good enough. Once you understand the root cause of this belief, you have the ability to delete it and add a new, loving script to your thoughts.

Internal dialog begins with the story you tell yourself. If you don't like the story, change it. In chapter 1, I gave the example of wallowing in sadness over lost love because feeling sadness had somehow justified the relationship's existence. I had experienced real love because I was now sad, a proclamation to the world that I had been in love. Once I acknowledged this was the core truth I was living into, I was then able to compassionately let go of it and rewrite a new story. If you have a hard time letting go of a story without filling it with a new program, then reframe the situation that caused your decision to feel a certain way, and make it positive. "I loved him and he loved me, and it ended peacefully."

One of my mottos is, 'self-talk yourself to a higher plane of existence'. I use power words that enable me to feel empowered. They're different for everyone. Depending on the situation, I may think vulnerability, transparency, strength, honor, kindness, or humble are power words. Our internal voice and recordings can be flipped to positive. You are a unique individual, finding the words that work for you will depend on your personal history, current situation and the goal or outcome you'd like to occur. For example, if I'm in business negotiations I'll be in a higher plane of existence internally if I focus on transparent, humble and honorable.

Let's focus on transparent; this doesn't mean I give all of the information away to my colleagues, but I will not believe I'm in a position to 'hide' information from them. People innately feel a threat response if they believe you are hiding something from them. It's how we're hardwired as humans, and people usually pick up on it, even if what we're hiding unrelated to the current conversation or situation you're in. Maybe you remember a time when a coworker slighted you in a meeting and that thought pops up when you speak with them. Of course you refrain from saying it, but the act of hiding it is usually perceived, and the level of trust they have for you will diminish.

Implementing positive power words into your mind will move your mind to a higher plane of existence. This layered with staying present and in the moment with people when you're having a conversation is one mindful way of avoiding thoughts about past experiences with them. When used together it enhances your relationship with yourself and others in a positive way.

Staying in the moment is also key when we think about our personal story. If you masterfully write your story that fits who you are today, and stop drudging up old hurts, you're able to move on in a joyful manner. Our personal story is the one we tell ourselves about ourselves. The 'I'm not good enough for x, y, z' or 'I'm getting fit' instead of 'I'm staying fit' or 'this job is beneath me, I deserve better'. Let's delve into the story we hold about our current job. I've worked in positions where I was the lowest woman on the totem pole, working around all the holidays because I lacked seniority and getting stuck doing the jobs that required very little brain function – if you know what I mean. Because I thought it was beneath me, I also wrote in my story that it was demeaning to do this work. That was a heavy load to carry around within myself, and depressing!

Now, I would tell my younger self to see every day as an opportunity to learn and grow. I am a leader in my life, it's my choice to be here doing this work. When it's mind numbingly boring I can hatch my plans for the business I've always wanted to start. I enjoy hard work; it makes me feel successful no matter the task. Finishing the task is even more rewarding, I could be completing dishes and I feel like I've won the lottery. That's a bit extreme, but you get my meaning. It's important to expose self-worth in the story you tell yourself:

working hard feels good, completing tasks is even better, it's my choice to work here, and I like it.

Key Learning

Shift internal dialog to shift emotions, our internal voice and recordings can be flipped to positive ones

Step 1

- o Feel how you feel in that moment of sadness or stress
- o Compassionately release the emotion(s) & then
- o Fill that space with an enjoyable emotion of your choice

Step 2

- o Ask yourself questions as you look at an area where you feel you're not good enough
- o Understand the root cause of this belief
- o Delete the old story
- o Add a new, loving script to your thoughts
- o Resetting yourself and your thought process when in a negative mood
- o Use your mantra "I am joyful, I am positive" or "I am enough" or something else you enjoy saying

- Use your physical presence – by this I mean smiling, relaxing tense muscles in our body and the tension on our face

This will impact how we interact with the world moving forward, without that yucky negative residue from previous encounters.

Through containing, or even better, releasing your negative experience from the morning, you'll do no harm to others.

Internal language is powerful – choose your words wisely
- Acknowledge the feeling of sadness attached to the disappointment and then let it go.
- Fill your mind with joyful thoughts about the task you decided to do (instead of working out).

*It is key to feel how you feel, release it and then fill that space with a new uplifting emotion.

Chapter 4: WHOLENESS
embracing your existence as a higher being

Once you set in motion a higher minded state of being coming from your internal dialog and personal story you are free to embrace your existence as a higher being, and live a positive life inside your minds, as well as externally.

Choose to embrace yourself as a higher minded being. Buy into it, sell it to yourself, and give it away to others. In chapter 2 we discussed reframing who you've become to loved ones, helping them to see you differently. In the beginning you may find it important to talk with loved ones, compassionately reaffirm with them when they refer to your behavior set in an old story you've grown out of, and define yourself outwardly as a verbal affirmation.

The most liberating part for me was embracing myself as a higher minded being. Stating affirmations is helpful and repetition enables our brains to ingrain the new message in our thoughts. As mentioned in Chapter 2, here's a couple simple mantra I found empowering that you may choose to use, or choose one of your liking if this doesn't resonate with you.

I am positive. I am joyful.

OR

I am enough (by Marisa Peer)

Buy into it, sell it to yourself and give it away to others for free. As mentioned in Chapter 3, our mind doesn't know the difference between our reality and our imagination. The beliefs we place in our mind shift our perception of reality. The more we believe something, the more it is ingrained in our being and shows up in our life. Repetition helps to absorb a new concept or a shift in our perception. Using daily mantras enables the message to get into our DNA, at an energy, and soul level. When my mind shifts to a thought or a feeling that I'm not willing to buy into, I say affirmations such as, 'I am positive' and 'I am joyful'. We buy into it and sell it to ourselves.

Giving it away to others is referred to in Chapter 2. We can choose to respond in a positive way to difficult people or loved ones by sharing our joyful selves more fully. When we lift others up into a positive light, we receive the gift of feeling good. It's a bit selfish sounding but that's how it works. We feel better when we share positivity with others. It's embodying and embracing your existence as your highest self and sharing this gift with others, and it feels rewarding.

As Gandhi once wrote: Thoughts Become Things...

Your beliefs become your thoughts,

Your thoughts become your words,

Your words become your actions,

Your actions become your habits,

Your habits become your values,

Your values become your destiny.

In other words....

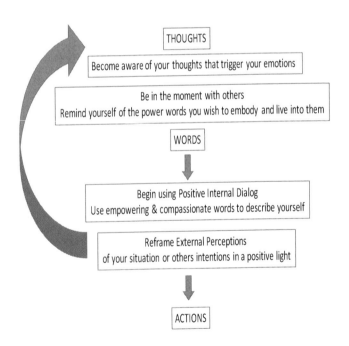

Positive breeds positive. We've all witnessed negative breeds negative, we can flip it and reverse the cycle. There are times when I'm in a room with colleagues who are miserable on Mondays. Every week it's the same grunts and groans from co-workers, wishing they were at home or anywhere else they can think of. This is a toxic environment if we allow ourselves to fall into the trap and join in the commiserating. To combat this cycle in our work culture, a fellow co-worker -- who happened to be a charming older gentlemen, who if you spoke with him you'd learn all about his family who he loved dearly -- made a t-shirt which had 'Happy Monday' written in bright yellow above a picture of his smiling face on its front. He came to work every Monday wearing that t-shirt. It was a beautiful statement and others followed suit saying 'Happy Monday' while walking down the hallway. The smallest acts of positivity can have a massive impact.

His sentiment lives in many of us to this day. Maybe you won't make a t-shirt, but you could start your own 'Happy Monday' campaign at work by simply smiling and holding your joyful space, inviting others to interact. In doing this you're creating a positive space for folks and a chance to mirror the positivity, adding to the greater good of your community at work.

When we act out of thinking of the greater good and doing no harm to others, it shifts our perception of next steps in situations and allows space for positivity and joy to enter more fluidly. A greater good doesn't have to be personal or about an individual person or a 'Happy Monday' t-shirt. But it's powerful, look at the ripple effect each person has, and on every person they come in contact with, in one day. It has a multiplying effect or ripple effect! Be mindful that how we impact each person, who then impacts 10 more people, sometimes all stems from one interaction. Have you ever had a hard conversation, and it didn't go the way you planned, or the outcome was unexpected? Resetting ourselves and our thought process, using our mantra or physical presence – by this I mean smiling, relaxing tense muscles in our body and the tension on our face – will impact how we interact moving forward, without that yucky negative residue from previous encounters. Through containing, or even better, releasing your negative experience from the morning, you'll do no harm to others.

Another way to view others who are in a negative space is to think of them as a living in their own personal bubble that doesn't affect us in any way. It's the same bubble many of us used to live in, the one where we thought about small problems endlessly, fixated on the past or future or even imagining scenario's that may or may not occur. Most of the time what folks are thinking about is out of their control and not worthy of their time and attention, only adding stress & negativity to their day: "I wonder what so and so meant by that statement, was he slighting me?", "Do I look okay?", "I don't like this shirt I'm wearing", "I need to do my nails", "I need to work out", "I wonder what so-and-so thinks of what I said", "Why is this car in front of me driving so slow". Then imagine we are in a positive thought bubble and reframe those drivers around us. Once we can compassionately reframe the other person or people, we are able to move our thoughts beyond this negative energy sucking model and shift to our higher self, where we are positive and joyful.

When I'm driving I imagine the other drivers who are driving slow with a new born baby in the backseat or maybe they had a hard day at the office or got some bad news or even simply having compassion and mercy towards drivers knowing that I will have slower reflexes some day and will drive slower in order to be extremely cautious not to get in an accident. Thinking of the greater good may be as simple as knowing there's another way to live and it's your choice to live it. Doing no harm to others may simply be acknowledging other's patterns compassionately, and at the same time, maintaining your own positive patterns and space.

Developing a spacious, free existence with wholeness at its core is done while owning our joyful presence no matter who or what you come into contact with. It sounds like a lot to bite off, but let me give you an example and then break it down into bite size steps.

Let's start with our body, the external presence we show the world, and the premise that our minds respond to the physical. When stressful situations arise, moving us to a negative thought process, we tend to have a physical reaction to our internal thoughts. If you notice how your body reacts in these situations you can unlearn the muscle memory you've held onto for ages.

Here is an exercise to try. Think of a time when you moved into a negative space, your boss told you off first thing in the morning, your coworker did that one thing that annoys you again, or you had an interaction with a difficult person at work. Relive that experience for a few seconds. Allow yourself to feel your muscles tense, maybe your face changes and scrunches up, your shoulders rise to your ears, your knees pull closer together, or any combination of these. Before letting go of the memory, completely tense your body, take a few breathes and then fully relax. When we have these experiences, it's like we're trying to hide inside ourselves and pull ourselves inward to our core. Now relax and let go of the memory. Move yourself to a power position, one where you're standing up straight, a smile on your face, hands on hips like Wonder Woman, chest high, chin down a little and then feel your feet firmly on the ground. Feel the empowered sensation of your body in this pose. Now try to relive the same memory. I bet it's impossible to feel as stressed while in this body pose. Our minds are impacted by our physical body. The way we stand, pose, or simply smile, impacts our brain's ability to feel emotions.

We innately tighten up when we feel stress or tension. If we allow ourselves to relax and fill the space in our thoughts with positive and joyful energy - that is ours naturally - we will develop a spacious, free existence with wholeness at its core.

Exercise Steps: Use your body to move you to a positive mental space
- Relive a memory that was stressful
- Hold that memory in your mind
- Notice your emotions
- Notice your body's reaction
- Tense up completely
- Take a few deep breaths
- Relax completely

- Move your body to a power position
- Relive the same memory

*Notice you're unable to feel as miserable as you were the first time. You've created a spacious existence to embrace the positive in this moment

Part of our existence as our higher self and creating wholeness is about celebrating! Joyously celebrating (yours and your friends) accomplishments no matter how small they may be. Honestly, the best medicine to becoming joyful is to joyously celebrate in any given moment.

Now, let's add an action to the thought! Embracing your new mantra, I AM JOYFUL, will be more effective once you add actions to the words. This daily task is a bridge, bringing joy into your everyday activates. Mindfully doing tasks brings us pleasure. Washing dishes, shaving, cooking food, or jogging/exercise are… all daily tasks we can embrace with celebration.

RECAP:

Beliefs → Thoughts → Words → Actions → Habits → Values → Destiny

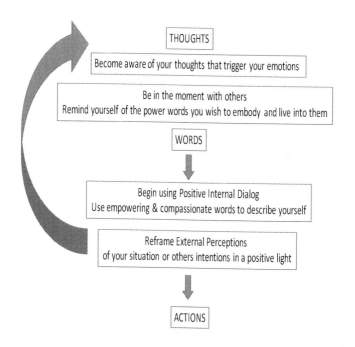

THOUGHTS

Become aware of your thoughts that trigger your emotions

Be in the moment with others
Remind yourself of the power words you wish to embody and live into them

WORDS

Begin using Positive Internal Dialog
Use empowering & compassionate words to describe yourself

Reframe External Perceptions
of your situation or others intentions in a positive light

ACTIONS

One practice is to do tasks mindfully with the intention of being JOYFUL Let's take washing dishes as an example. Before beginning, move your body to a power position, discussed earlier in this chapter. Standing firmly on the ground, chest high, back straight, with a partial smile on your face take in the area where you'll begin the task. Perhaps the first step is surveying the house for rogue glasses or taking into account how full the dish drainer is and putting the clean dishes in their proper place. Run the water at the perfect temperature you enjoy to do dishes at, adding your favorite soap, perhaps smelling it first (noticing how you enjoy the scent and it's comforting aroma), or placing it in your hands to feel how its texture (familiar to the touch, all the while smiling).

Then, I tend to place the glasses in the hot sudsy water first, rolling them back and forth a bit so they have a chance to be fully covered by hot water; washing each cup thoroughly (perhaps thinking of when you bought them and how joyful you were to find that perfect color), wiping the sides, bottom and inside with my favorite dishcloth (smiling as I think how efficient the dishcloth is and how I like the color of the cloth). I set them aside and rinse all at once, so as not to waste water. Then carefully place them in the drying rack, leaving room for other dishes. And so on, until you've completed the entire load. Then remembering to stay in your power position, take a moment to acknowledge the task is accomplished & that you feel joyful.

Exercise steps, Mindfully do a task:

- Move your body to a power position and try to hold a variation of it while doing the task if possible
- Observe surroundings, the lay of the land before beginning, see things where they are
- Fully experience each step of the task to be accomplished
- Smile while doing the task
- Bring forth positive thoughts while doing the task, enjoy it!
- Allow for a moment of satisfaction once the task is complete

The more often we bring our new mantra I AM POSITIVE, I AM JOYFUL or I AM ENOUGH into our thoughts and deeds, they in turn will become habit. Celebrating the process of accomplishing our daily tasks becomes a backdrop for our minds to settle into when in the resting state, your new destiny is a joyful one!

Key Learning

Choose a mantra that resonates with your true nature, joyful:

I AM JOYFUL

I AM POSITIVE

I AM ENOUGH or choose another to your liking

Ideas to reflect on:

- Positive breeds positive
- Stay close to the positive people in your life
- Positive ripple effect, think of a higher good & do no harm to others
- Fill your space with positive & joyful energy
- Celebrate your Mantra, mindfully and compassionately
- Embrace your highest self and openly share your mindset with others, (revisited from Chapter 2)

Resetting ourselves and your thought process to do no harm to others

State your mantra I AM JOYFUL, I AM POSITIVE, I AM ENOUGH

o Adjust your physical presence – by this I mean: smiling, relaxing tense muscles in our body and the tension on our face. This will impact how we interact moving forward, without that yucky negative residue from previous encounters.

o Through containing, or even better, releasing your negative experience from the morning, you'll do no harm to others.

Rewrite your personal story

o Delete myths that no longer serve your intention to be joyful and positive

o If you don't like the story, change it

o Use power words in self-talk to move your mind to a higher plane of existence

o Masterfully rewrite your story, filling it with self-worth and positive language

Use your body to move you to a positive mental space

o Relive a memory that was stressful

o Hold that memory in your mind

o Notice your emotions

o Notice your body's reaction

o Tense up completely

o Take a few deep breaths

- Relax completely
- Move your body to a power position
- Exercise steps:
- Mindfully doing a task
- Move your body to a power position, & smile
- Relive the same memory
- Notice you're unable to feel as miserable as you were the first time
- You've created a spacious existence to embrace the positive in this moment

Backsliding Strategies

- Choose a mantra that resonates with you I AM JOYFUL, I AM POSITIVE
- Embrace your highest self and openly share your mindset with others
- Positive breads positive, stay close to the positive people in your life
- Positive ripple effect, think of a higher good & do no harm to others
- Filling your space with positive & joyful energy
- Celebrating your Mantra, mindfully

Chapter 5: CLEAR YOUR SPACE & THE CLUTTER
Simple and impactful meditation exercises

In this chapter we'll review a few simple and impactful meditation exercises. Meditation can be done in many forms, not all of them while sitting still. In chapter 4 we discovered how to mindfully complete daily tasks. If you find the meditation in this chapter doesn't resonate with you, replace it with mindfulness exercise in Chapter 4 or the smiling meditation. As the Dalai Lama said while on tour in 2015, "sometimes smiling is better than just meditating" When meditation doesn't work for you, smile. As we discussed in chapter 1, a wonderful way to bring a joyful and positive energy into every moment is by simply smiling.

The practice of smiling has scientific backing. There are feel good chemicals released by our brains when certain muscles are put in motion, and a smile is one of them. This does not mean I walk around grinning like a fool. Let's go over how to create a partial smile which will release this good energy and allow you to be taken seriously at work!

Exercise: Mindful Smile Meditation

- o Find a mirror
- o Get into your power pose
- o Relax your facial muscles, make a kissy face in the mirror, relax your face again
- o Open your eyes completely, as wide as possible, feel the muscles stretch, relax your face again
- o Smile as big as you are able, think a funny story or a funny picture or just fill with joy, relax your face again
- o Now smile big and open your eyes as wide as possible, look in the mirror, have a chuckle at the joyful surprise you'll see reflecting in the mirror
- o Relax your face muscles
- o Now smile slowly in front of the mirror, just until the corners of your mouth are upturned
- o If it's comfortable, open your eyes as if you're hearing the most interesting and hopeful story from a friend with much anticipation, as if you can't wait to hear what happens next

This is the facial position which will enhance your brain chemistry activity towards a joyful existence, as well as create a positive mental state. Somehow it's easier to maintain a positive mental state when you have a partial smile on your face

Now we'll move into an exercise which is a simple mindful meditation. The objective is to be present with yourself in a compassionate way, to love yourself. This exercise can be done in less than 5 minutes. If you're looking for a longer more in-depth meditation, there are many resources online. I suggest reviewing Shamash Alidina's Kindness Meditation on his site for guided meditations on kindness and compassion.

Exercise: Kindness Meditation

In this exercise we'll begin by giving ourselves compassion. When compassion and love begins at our center, it acts as a device to instill love and kindness in our interactions with others. We'll use the below script to practice. Sit comfortably, arms relaxed, eyes open or closed, whatever is more comfortable for you. It may take some time to settle down, breathe deeply through your nostrils for a few minutes, then move into the kindness portion of the below text.

- Breathe through your nose a few times
- Allow your body and mind to soften
- Feel your sit bones and relax even further
- Maybe there's a little more space in between your ears and shoulders
- Continue to breathe through your nose

- Allow yourself to become a little more centered with each breath
- Continue to breathe through your nose until you feel relaxed and centered in your body
- Now think of yourself
- Exhale and repeat I LOVE MYSELF
- Inhale and repeat I am free from suffering
- Inhale and repeat I am experiencing the highest form of happiness
- Inhale and repeat I am the embodiment of love
- Repeat the above twice
- Breathe through your nose a few times
- Allow your body and mind to soften
- Feel your sit bones and relax even further
- Maybe there's a little more space between your ears and shoulders
- Continue to breathe through your nose
- Allow yourself to become a little more centered with each breath
- Continue to breathe through your nose until you feel relaxed and centered in your body
- Gently come back to the present moment

The kindness meditation is a practice of self-love. Rarely do we send ourselves compassion and kindness, it's usually others we're thinking of. It's one of the practices you can use to remain in a joyful and positive mindset, especially when we slip a little and have a day when it's challenging to remain positive. In less than 5 minutes you have the ability to practice self-care and to nurture yourself in these trying moments. The longer you practice the meditation, the more quickly you'll feel the results of love and kindness for yourself. Removing expectations at the onset of the meditation will enable you to feel more fully the self-love and care you're providing for yourself when you're having a trying moment.

As time goes by and you instill these practices, it will become easier to reset yourself to a positive mindset or to simply to feel cared and loved in a trying moment. In either case, it's of value to have the singular outcome of self-love when practicing this meditation.

Key Learning

When challenging moments occur and your mood is down, flip the switch through self-care. Utilize the smiling meditation to enhance your mood in any moment

- o Find a mirror
- o Get into your power pose
- o Relax your facial muscles, make a kissy face in the mirror, relax your face again
- o Open your eyes completely, as wide as possible, feel the muscles stretch, relax your face again
- o Smile as big as you are able, think a funny story or a funny picture or just fill with joy, relax your face again
- o Now smile big and open your eyes as wide as possible, look in the mirror, have a chuckle at the joyful surprise you'll see reflecting in the mirror
- o Relax your face muscles
- o Now smile slowly in front of the mirror, just until the corners of your mouth are upturned
- o If it's comfortable, open your eyes as if you're hearing the most interesting and hopeful story from a friend with much anticipation, as if you can't wait to hear what happens next.

- This is the facial position which will enhance your brain chemistry activity towards a joyful existence, as well as create a positive mental state. Somehow it's easier to maintain a positive mental state when you have a partial smile on your face.

Share kindness and self-compassion to yourself to strengthen your mindset of joy and positivity

- Breathe through your nose a few times
- Allow your body and mind to soften
- Feel your sit bones and relax even further
- Maybe there's a little more space in between your ears and shoulders
- Continue to breathe through your nose
- Allow yourself to become a little more centered with each breath
- Continue to breathe through your nose until you feel relaxed and centered in your body
- Now think of yourself
- Exhale and repeat I LOVE MYSELF
- Inhale and repeat I am free from suffering
- Inhale and repeat I am experiencing the highest form of happiness
- Inhale and repeat I am the embodiment of love

Repeat the above twice

- Breathe through your nose a few times
- Allow your body and mind to soften
- Feel your sit bones and relax even further
- Maybe there's a little more space between your ears and shoulders
- Continue to breathe through your nose
- Allow yourself to become a little more centered with each breath
- Continue to breathe through your nose until you feel relaxed and centered in your body
- Gently come back to the present moment

Backsliding Strategies

- When challenging moments occur and your mood is down, flip the switch through self-care
- Utilize the smiling meditation to enhance your mood in any moment
- Share kindness and self-compassion to yourself to strengthen your mindset of joyful and positive

Chapter 6: MINDFUL EXISTENCE
Be curious and playful in the process

Maintaining a curious and playful nature while in the process of transformation takes stress out of the equation or at least minimizes it. To some, it may feel a bit loaded to say I am now positive and joyful. Like it's a mountain we're climbing and at the end of it we'll be in this enlightened state of joy and bliss. It's not so. There are steps we can take to shift our mindset, as we have read in previous chapters, but there is also an innate way to go about making changes. A playful, curious mindset enables us to grasp new ideas and new ways of being! Just as school age children learn new concepts in class, we as adults have the ability to absorb and transform into whatever we like.

Do you recall a crucial moment just before reacting or getting carried away in a conversation, when you knew you could remedy the situation or shift the mood of the conversation by responding differently than you have in the previous moments? This is the moment, if you're able, it's the best time to infuse a playful or curious nature. Laughing diffuses social awkwardness and alleviates stressful situations. It's not always possible to be funny on cue, it's a challenge for me as well. The point is to revert your face to the semi-smile when in these crucial moments of make it or break it, when you want to shift to a positive mindset.

The second thing to do is breathe! So often we get use to a tightness in our face and chest, it exemplifies an internal struggle or fight to hold on. If we can ask open ended questions in conversations, and allow others to say what they are intending, it is much easier for us to respond in a way that allows us to maintain our positive and joyful nature. Look, life is not always going to allow us to be happy go lucky, but our internal state is ours to manage. By making a choice to be curious, we have already shifted the paradigm we have allowed to happen for years.

When a difficult conversation arises where you tend to tense up and shift to a less than enjoyable state of mind, try asking open ended questions to the person you're speaking with. At the very least, this will allow you a moment to shift your face to the semi-smile and your body to a power position. Doing this allows your physical stance to support a positive mindset. In my experience, when I ask open ended questions, the person I'm in a conversation with will relax and begin to open up a bit as they discuss their topic in a non-judgmental environment, with me positioning myself to shift into a positive mindset. Becoming curious and inviting others to express themselves freely allows me time to anchor into a positive mental state (through the presence of breath or your physical stature) so I'm able to respond rather than react.

Exercise: Crucial moments in conversations when you want to shift to curious, playful and positive mindsets

- Add a semi-smile on your face
- Breath
- Shift your body to a power position
- Be curious, ask open ended questions to create a non-judgmental environment
- Anchor yourself into a positive mental state through the presence of breath or your physical stature

A playful anecdote one client recently mentioned was that in the past he was an overtly aggressive driver, beeping at people who tried to cut in and angry at other drivers when they didn't follow his etiquette on the road. You know the type of driver he was, knuckles gripping the steering wheel, weaving in and out of traffic. He said it was because he was an over achiever. All of his friends that were over achievers drove the same way and he wrote it off as normal. Then he added a bit of playfulness and curiosity into his life. At one point he wanted to know what it was like to drive as a different person. Why were these other drivers smiling while in the car? What was he missing out on?

He made it into a game, he decided to create a different persona while driving! For a time, he pretended to be someone else. While driving, he imagined his Grandpa, who had attributes such as patience, generosity, and kindness. He allowed others to go in front of him in rush hour traffic. He didn't beep at the car next to him that was a centimeter too close. He said at the end of the drive he felt more relaxed, joyful, and able to focus on whatever his next task was in the day. He was surprised at this outcome. For the most part he said he's let go of the angry person he became in the car, but there are days when he still drives like what I would call a maniac. The end result may not be what we thought, and the path to get there may not be what we think it is either. As we mentioned in chapter 2, Choose Empowerment, we spoke of how our brains and body at a primal state are hardwired to go to the negative. If we consciously shift to a positive state of mind in a playful and curious way, we enable new possibilities to arise.

Exercise: Add playfulness to stressful moments
- o   While driving Pretended to be someone else while driving imagined your Grandparent

- Take on their attributes - such as patience, generosity, and kindness
- Continue to drive and see if you enjoy this experience
- Change-up which happy person you pretend to be while driving to see if there are different results

We have the ability to develop and create ourselves as we wish to exist. In any given moment you and I can choose to be who we want to be, no matter what we have done in the past, what decisions we have made or the previous context of a relationship. We can and do choose to create ourselves. This book is about making the shift to a joyful and positive presence and acknowledging the moments when we are not representing ourselves in a kind manner is of value. These are the moments when we do not want to beat ourselves up, when we may practice the kindness meditation from Chapter 5 and love ourselves. There is great learning in these moments, and it's an opportunity to develop new patterns of how you respond to situations or past triggers. We'll look at these more thoroughly in this chapter. First, let's add playfulness and creativity to developing who we are.

One client told me she wanted to surprise her husband. In all the years they had been married, she had responded to him being late for any event with frustration, taking it as a personal affront. You can imagine the persona she had created surrounding his tardiness. At some point she was tired of responding in a negative way, and she wished to embrace this annoyance with a joyful presence. It was bringing her down to relive this old persona that no longer fit her mental state. So, the next time her husband arrived later than expected, she decided to be open and loving with him. She met him in her power position body pose and with the warmth of a semi-smile, gave him a hug and a kiss, and then sincerely asked if "everything was alright dear?". It was her ideal blend of confidence and femininity. She mentioned his surprise and how he was more relaxed and seemed to enjoyed himself more at the event after the welcome he received.

It positively impacts our relationships if we share a joyful presence when it's most difficult for us to muster up the joy! The concept is similar to Chapter 4, Wholeness, when we spoke of buying into, selling, and giving away for free the idea that we choose to embrace ourselves as higher minded beings. The more we give away our positive and joyful presence, the more we are met with this same mindset; like attracts like.

Exercise: Choose to create ourselves

- First observe your patterns, what persona have you been living into
- Where you can improve your responses
- Develop and create yourself as you wish to be
- Add self-love through the kindness meditation
- Create who you want to be in every given moment, no matter what your past decisions have been

Compassion for yourself goes a long way in self-discovery and redefining yourself. Sometimes it's of value to give compassion to the person you're in a relationship with to move forward and evolve your persona to one you wish to create.

I have struggled with having an irritable response to people who gossip. It was a trigger for me and I wasn't enjoying the person I became and my reactions to gossipers. So I decided to flip the switch to a more positive and joyful self through acknowledging my response. I lent myself compassion, giving compassion to the other person or rather the trigger, reframed the trigger – defusing the point at which I became irritable, and created the positive and joyful persona I wished to embrace.

There was a gossiper at a company I used to work for. It used to annoy me to no end when folks speak unkind about others. My mind goes directly to judgments like: 'there's always two sides to the story", "I'm seeing the ugly in you right now", and "Be kind, it's so much more becoming of you". Then I realized that I was responding in an irritable way to people who were gossiping. My own judgments were a reflection of myself, not the other person, and it was not the person I wanted to be in those moments. So I found a way to switch it up and stay in an empathic listening frame of mind when I encounter gossipers. I created compassion for myself, yup, it's a trigger for me when people gossip and I acknowledge this about myself with kindness and love. Self-love helped me let go of becoming irritable when I felt it happening the next time.

As a second step I decided to reframe gossiping. It's sometimes a way for people to safely release tepid feelings without eventually blowing up and saying hurtful things to others. I think of it as kettle blowing off steam, once done, the steam is gone and you're left with temped water. This does not mean I listen for hours on end to gossip, rather I have patience & compassion for myself. When gossip shows up, if it lasts too long, I am vocal about it making me uncomfortable to hear, then together we move on to the next subject in our conversation naturally, and I preserve my mental status.

Moving through triggers that elicit our own unwelcomed reactions

- o Acknowledge the reaction you've had
- o Add compassion internally to yourself, be kind to yourself and don't beat yourself up
- o Reframe the trigger externally, this adds compassion to the people you're interacting with
- o Move on, responding from the positive and joyful persona you are embracing

There's an upside to using compassion. Once I no longer reacted to folks gossiping, I was then thought of by my colleague as having patience and was trusted me more because I heard their story without judgement which they may have interpreted as buying into who was right or wrong. I listened placidly as a contemporary, and they knew I would lend the same courtesy if another coworker complained to me about them, which is reassuring and builds bonds. So compassion enhanced my relationships at work.

Acknowledge your external triggers and lend compassion to yourself internally so you may have more fruitful relationships with your colleagues. Other people have ways of dealing with their stress that may not jive with you or your true nature.

If you struggle to find compassion for the other person so that you may move forward through the situation, try a visualization exercise. We're adding external compassion by imagining the person's past, imagine their present – put yourself in their place, see through their eyes, imagine what they might be feeling right now. Through this process of imagery, stuff may come up and there may be anger, though the longer that you do this imagery, the more these feelings will dissipate. Compassion usually starts with ourselves and acts as a device to instill kindness into our relationships.

Key Learning:

Crucial moments in conversations when you want to shift to curious, playful and positive mindsets:

- o Add a semi-smile on your face
- o Breath
- o Shift your body to a power position
- o Be curious, ask open ended questions to create a non-judgmental environment
- o Anchor yourself into a positive mental state through the presence of breath or your physical stature

Add playfulness to stressful moments while driving

- o Pretended to be someone else while driving

- Imagined your Grandparent
- Take on their attributes such as patience, generosity, and kindness
- Continue to drive and see if you enjoy this experience
- Change-up which happy person you pretend to be while driving to see if there are different results

Choose to create ourselves and our persona

- First observe your patterns, what persona have you been living into
- Where you can improve your responses
- Develop and create yourself as you wish to be
- Add self-love through the kindness meditation
- Create who you want to be in every given moment, no matter what your past decisions have been

Moving through triggers that elicit reactions not responses

- Acknowledge the response you've had
- Add compassion internally to yourself, be kind to yourself and don't beat yourself up
- Reframe the trigger externally, this adds compassion to the people you're interacting with
- Move on, creating a positive and joyful persona you wish to embrace

Visualization exercise

- o Add external compassion by imagining the person's past, imagine their present – put yourself in their place, see through their eyes, imagine what they might be feeling right now
- o Compassion usually starts with ourselves and acts as a device to instill kindness into our relationships

Chapter 7: FINDING LIKE-MINDED PEOPLE
Build a community

Building a community of like-minded people is of value when we're in a transformative state. Moving from one friend group to another completely may not be what you envision for yourself, or be realistic. It is possible to integrate new friends into your current circles if you're concerned about leaving relationships behind. This chapter isn't about letting go of your social circle; it's about enhancing your life and building a foundation for successful change.

"Some people are here for a lifetime, a day, a year or a season..."

Being around like-minded people provides affirmation and support on a very base level. It enables us to have a stronger sense of self because we have others around to mirror the traits we wish to emulate. In Chapter 1 we discussed mirroring body language and in chapter 4 mirroring behavior. When these concepts are coupled in your daily life, it's powerful and impactful to support your mindset and decision to be joyful and positive.

Research shows that we are the sum of the 5 people we spend the most time with. For this reason, it's of value to find like-minded people. Like attracts like, spend time around like minded people and sustain well-being with ease. Choose otherwise and it may be a struggle and unsustainable. Bottom line, build a community filled with constructive & meaningful relationships.

Another technique I found helpful in order to keep a joyful presence is laughter and celebrating. It's like this; if we choose to celebrate ours and our friend's accomplishments, no matter how small they are, we are staying present in a positive & joyful mindset. It isn't necessary to leave behind all relationships you already have but to mindfully create new ones and begin to shift the ones you have to be born from a constructive and meaningful basis.

Another tool is to celebrate and find laughter. As you can imagine, at first, this didn't come naturally. I had a serious persona at work, with very little colleagues I called friends, until I decided I wanted to enjoy my work and my life more. It was a little weird for me, as well as for my colleagues, for me to behave a bit more lighthearted before and after meetings. Or when walking down the hallway, remembering to be present and see who was around me, stopping and saying a cheery hello, instead of walking stern faced as if I'm on a mission to my next engagement. Once I loosened up a bit, my colleagues loosened up as well. It was like an iceberg had melted between us and I was ready for the relationships and our conversations to shift to a more joyful tone.

I still had all of the workload and responsibility to manage, but I was enjoying my time at the office and the people I was working with. The more time passed and everyone was sure this enhanced likable persona was going to stick, people began trusting me differently and having lighthearted joyful conversations. At the onset, I initiated the celebratory tone of conversations with folks. I trained myself and others that it was okay to express this joy. Layering in being grateful for the feeling of joy or practice being grateful for these moments, events, friends and loved ones which leave you feeling joy is a powerful tool to engrain into the DNA level so it is a part of how we are naturally.

I had to be open to the change and be the change before others were able to express themselves in a joyful manner while with me. Layering in being grateful, had the effect of detaching from any expectations that my joyful attitude would yield a specific result with colleagues or how they viewed me. To a certain extent, I was the problem. I didn't need to go find a new job with better people, what I needed to do was loosen up and laugh more at work, creating space for others to bring their joyful presence into the conversations. I'm not one for looking back and being embarrassed by my old habits, I find it much better to stay present in the moment with who I am today.

Through my mindfulness practice I knew I had to find ways to leave the past in the past and stay in the present moment. I'll admit that it was tough to not get a little embarrassed at my behavior before switching my new joyful M.O., especially when colleagues would give me a double take after we shared a laugh, with an expression of "who are you & what happened to that all-business lady you use to be".

In the end, by choosing to be a person who laughs and celebrates, I drew out this trait in others that were already around me.

Use power words when speaking to others, choose otherwise and it will be a struggle. In Chapter 4 we spoke of Gandhi's quote, thoughts become words and words become actions. The reverse it also true. The words we use impact our subconscious mind and how we view our immediate environment. If we speak in positive tones, our perceptions of reality shift to positive. Now I'm not saying run around like Pollyanna, there's always the ability to be realistic and grounded while remaining positive. It's a balance that some people need to figure out, but it's possible and rewarding once you do.

As I mentioned in Chapter 3, I'm a jogger and used to say that I needed to "get" in shape instead of stating it more accurately and uplifting - I'm "staying" in shape. For me this slight change of wording was a game changer.

Again, our brains don't know the difference between our reality and our imagination

By detaching my mind from the negative connotation of words used to describe my current situation, I was able to navigate each moment viewed in a more positive light and mindset. Staying present in the moment and aware of the words we use is powerful in switching our minds to a stable positive resting place.

Some of the usual suspects in my vernacular were:
- This is Difficult -> This is Challenging
- I need x -> I want x
- I will -> wouldn't it be nice
- I'm getting in shape -> I'm staying in shape

- I fear an outcome ☾ I have a plan to navigate the outcome I fear
- I have to get this work done NOW ☾ I have time to engage with my colleagues joyfully, smile and say hello
- I'm slacking off right now ☾ I'm engaging with playfulness that helps me be more productive after I allow myself this outlet
- I have no idea why this person is saying this ☾ what questions can I ask to better understand their perspective

In reference to the language we use, it's important to remember that not only how we speak out loud to others is valuable, but the internal dialog and thought process we allow is equally valuable. Fear was one of the biggest root causes of the negative language I used internally. As we mentioned in Chapter 1, once we find the root cause, we are then able to reframe the situation and move forward with the emotion we choose to embrace.

In reference to fear as a root cause as it pertains to self-sabotage; I began to think of fear as a powerful tool. If I'm afraid of an outcome, then I am able to map out the path that would happen if my fear came true; when I make decisions, what are the possible products of each decision which leads down the path I am afraid of. Once I know what the possible paths are if my fears come true, then I comprise a plan to navigate and make sure those outcomes don't come to fruition. If one of my fears does come into reality, I have thought through the process and have the ability to create other avenues to move to the positive end goal that I have imagined. I no longer self-sabotage with internal dialog which is not in line with the positive outcomes I wish to see happen in my life.

Lean into the relationships you've nurtured with like-minded people. I have created an accountability group with folks who are seeking similar goals, we meet together once a week online to celebrate your victories and gain valuable feedback along the way. Your group doesn't have to be based on being joyful and positive… although that is a very cool concept.. it could be a group that has a similar hobby or activity that you all enjoy. We are a group of heart centered, spiritual business women who are working to be of service and help others with our mission driven businesses and products. We all have a unique journey, history and presence which lends to variations on self-awareness, thought patterns and emotional intelligence. There would be a void in my life without a group like this. We can learn lessons without living them ourselves, if we engage and listen with our hearts to our tribe. This is a value of building a community least spoken about – learning through others mishaps. Look we're all in it together ultimately, share your joyful self and practice self-care for your thoughts. Our compassion for ourselves and others ultimately will lead to a positive life experience and this doesn't mean be a push over. We still should be mindful to get our work done and fight for injustices when able.

Our time together is coming to a close, I am grateful to have been a part of your life and it is my hope to have fulfilled my mission to be of service to you. This body of work is near and dear to my heart. Many of my life's lessons (sometimes painful) engrained these lessons into my DNA. I am grateful for your time and attention. Please be compassionate to yourselves if you backslide. Notice what you're thinking at that moment and switch your thinking. Don't be too hard on yourself for getting off course for a moment. We are the sum total of ourselves, not an individual moment. And you are able to be your joyful self with a positive mindset in this moment, no matter what... Simply Flip the switch.

Key Learning:

Create a community from your current network

- o Choose to be a person who laughs and celebrates with your current network

- This draws out this trait in others that are already around you
- Stay in the present and be mindful not to dwell on your past behavior
- Be grateful for the positive people in your life
- Enjoy yourself as you embody joyful behaviors

Use your fear to flip the switch for a different end result
- Define the outcome you're afraid of
- Map the steps or decisions that would occur for this outcome to come to fruition
- Proactively navigate and take actions which ensure the feared outcome doesn't occur
- If one fear comes to reality, I'll have thought through it and create a new avenue to circumvent it from moving any further forward in my reality
- No longer self-sabotage my life through my decisions and actions
- Remove negative connotations from your internal and external language
- Become mindful of the language you use in your mind and that you use when speaking

Replace words with negative connotations, with positive ones

- This is Difficult -> This is Challenging
- I need x -> I want x
- I will -> wouldn't it be nice
- I'm getting in shape -> I'm staying in shape
- I fear an outcome -> I have a plan to navigate the outcome I fear

Building a plan to navigate feared outcomes:

- Write the outcome I fear most
- Map out the path that would happen if my fear came true (when I make decisions, what are the possible products of each decision which leads down the path I am afraid of)
- Map out ways to go around it from happening
- When you see something pop up that you mapped out, do the thing you planned to have the desired outcome
- If one of my fears does come into reality, I have thought through the process and have the ability to create other avenues to move to the positive end goal that I have imagined

Infuse celebrating and Laughter in your life:

- It's the little things that bring joy, celebrate them at every opportunity

- Practice being grateful for these moments, events, friends and loved ones
- Laugh more often & use the smile meditation to get your mindset joyful
- Teach others that it's normal to be joyful when you meet at work or in your personal life
- Smile at work, remove the stern 'all business' face mask
- Say hello to colleagues

Be Mindfully aware of others:
- Walk down the hallway mindfully, be aware of who is around and say hello to them
- Create light-hearted dialog and create friendly relationships before meetings and at the end of the workday
- Detach from any expectations that your joyful attitude will yield a result with colleagues and you'll see more results

Stay Present:
- Don't look back or be embarrassed by your old habits, stay present in the moment with who you are today.
- Surround yourself with like-minded people
- Acknowledge yourself as a joyful positive person and find other like-minded people

- o Build a community filled with constructive & meaningful relationships
- o Create an accountability or mastermind group with like-minded folks who are seeking similar goals
- o Meet regularly, listen from a heart centered space and focus on being present

Backsliding:
- o Be compassionate to yourselves if you backslide and try not to beat yourself up or dwell on it
- o Notice what you're thinking as soon as you you're feeling off
- o Flip the switch to your joyful self with a positive mindset using the tools we discussed

SUMMARY

Flip the Switch Key Learning Takeaways

CHAPTER 1: PEACEFULNESS
Calm your mind and thoughts with compassion

Be compassionate with your mind and its racing thoughts:

- o Write down tasks
- o Be grateful to your mind for staying on the ball
- o Give permission to your mind to relax
- o Allow a sense of calm to overcome you

Own your decision to feel a certain way & flip the switch to a joyful existence:

- o Compassionately acknowledge you've embraced an emotion or thought process
- o Fill your personal space with joyful bodily expressions like smiling and positive thoughts.
- o Find the root cause or belief of why I'm embracing sadness and wallowing
- o Rethink its rationality
- o Reframe the situation that caused your decision to feel a certain way, make it positive

- o And moved on with the emotion you choose to fill your head space

Mindful Next Steps for Backsliding:
- o Free oneself from the overwhelmed state of mind
- o Slow things down, invoke calm thoughts in your life
- o Do the next thing that makes sense and do it mindfully
- o Move forward through personal choices of your emotional mindset

CHAPTER 2: CHOOSE EMPOWERMENT
Declare a positive and joyful existence

Joyful & Positive Naturally Tips Overview:
- o Make a conscious decision to be joyful and positive, it's in your nature
- o Flip the switch to positive when you backslide
- o Check in with yourself
- o Allow yourself to hear what others say to you in a positive tone and respond accordingly
- o Initiate mirroring positive body language and facial expressions
- o Own it you've earned it, allow yourself to believe you're positive and joyful

90/10 rule, create a story or word for a difficult person which enables you to have positive thoughts about them while interacting together

90/10 switching from 100% jerk
- Compassionately imagine the person has characteristics or values you positively identify with
- Create a story around the person that allows you to find reason to like them
- Envision the story before or during interactions with them to shift your thoughts about them to a more positive light
  OR
- Find a word that brings about compassion for the person who is difficult to deal with
- Use the word as a mantra when interacting with them to shift your thinking about them to the positive

Reframe yourself to others with compassion
- Be open and share your internal process of change and growth with the external world
- Vocally share a reframing of yourself when you feel labeled with the 'old you' by others
- Honor the person you were and the person you've become with compassion

- Have compassion for the people around you, changing how you're seen externally takes time

CHAPTER 3: BE MASTERFUL IN WRITING YOUR STORY
Choose language mindfully

Shift internal dialog to shift emotions, our internal voice and recordings can be flipped to positive ones

Step 1.
- Feel how you feel in that moment of sadness or stress. Compassionately release the emotion(s) & then fill that space with an enjoyable emotion of your choice

Step 2.
- Ask yourself questions as you look at an area where you feel you're not good enough
- Understand the root cause of this belief
- Delete the old story
- Add a new, loving script to your thoughts

Resetting yourself and your thought process when in a negative mood
- Use your mantra "I am joyful, I am positive" or "I am enough" or something else you enjoy saying

- o Use your physical presence – by this I mean smiling, relaxing tense muscles in our body and the tension on our face
- o This will impact how we interact with the world moving forward, without that yucky negative residue from previous encounters.
- o Through containing, or even better, releasing your negative experience from the morning, you'll do no harm to others

Internal language is powerful – choose your words wisely
- o Acknowledge the feeling of sadness attached to the disappointment and then let it go.
- o Fill your mind with joyful thoughts about the task you decided to do (instead of working out).

*It is key to feel how you feel, release it and then fill that space with a new uplifting emotion.

If you don't' like the story change it
- o Masterfully rewrite your story, filling it with self-worth and positive language
- o Delete myths that no longer serve your intention to be joyful and positive
- o Language is powerful – choose your words wisely

CHAPTER 4: WHOLENESS
Embracing your existence

Choose a mantra to repeat "I am positive; I am joyful"

Exercise Steps:

- o Relive a memory that was stressful
- o Hold that memory in your mind
- o Notice your emotions
- o Notice your body's reaction
- o Tense up completely
- o Take a few deep breaths
- o Relax completely
- o Move your body to a power position

Exercise steps: Mindfully doing a task

- o Move your body to a power position and try to hold a variation of it while doing the task if possible
- o Observe surroundings, the lay of the land before beginning, see things where they are
- o Fully experience each step of the task to be accomplished
- o Smile while doing the task
- o Bring forth positive thoughts while doing the task, enjoy it!

- Allow for a moment of satisfaction once the task is complete

Mindful Mantra:

- Choose a mantra that resonates with you I AM JOYFUL; I AM POSITIVE or I AM ENOUGH
- Embrace your highest self and openly share your mindset with others
- Positive breads positive, stay close to the positive people in your life
- Positive ripple effect, think of a higher good & do no harm to others
- Filling your space with positive & joyful energy
- Celebrating your Mantra, mindfully

Beliefs → Thoughts → Words → Actions → Habits → Values → Destiny

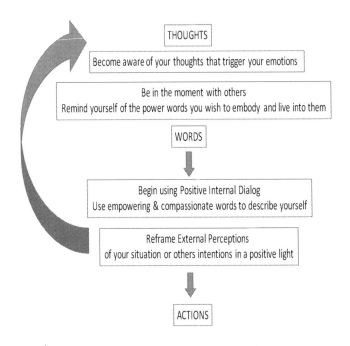

THOUGHTS

Become aware of your thoughts that trigger your emotions

Be in the moment with others
Remind yourself of the power words you wish to embody and live into them

WORDS

Begin using Positive Internal Dialog
Use empowering & compassionate words to describe yourself

Reframe External Perceptions
of your situation or others intentions in a positive light

ACTIONS

CHAPTER 5: CLEAR YOUR SPACE & THE CLUTTER
Simple and impactful meditation exercises

Exercise: Kindness meditation – adding self-compassion to your daily routine. As time goes by and you instill all of these practices, it will become easier to reset yourself to a positive mindset or to simply to feel yourself care and love in a trying moment.

Mindful Smile Meditation:

- o Find a mirror
- o Get in to your power pose
- o Relax your facial muscles, make a kissy face in the mirror, relax your face again
- o Open your eyes completely, as wide as possible, feel the muscles stretch, relax your face again
- o Smile as big as you are able, think a funny story or a funny picture or just fill with joy, relax your face again
- o Now smile big and open your eyes as wide as possible, look in the mirror, have a chuckle at the joyful surprise you'll see reflecting in the mirror
- o Relax your face muscles
- o Now smile slowly in front of the mirror, just until the corners of your mouth are upturned
- o If it's comfortable, open your eyes as if you're hearing the most interesting story from a friend

This is the facial position which will enhance your brain chemistry activity towards a joyful existence as well as create a mental state which is positive. Somehow it's easier to maintain a positive mental state when you have a partial smile on your face.

Self-care:

When challenging moments occur and your mood is down, flip the switch through self-care

- o Utilize the smiling meditation to enhance your mood in any moment
- o Share kindness and self-compassion to yourself to strengthen your mindset of joyful and positive

Share kindness and self-compassion to yourself to strengthen your mindset of joy and positivity

- o Breathe through your nose a few times
- o Allow your body and mind to soften
- o Feel your sit bones and relax even further
- o Maybe there's a little more space in between your ears and shoulders
- o Continue to breathe through your nose
- o Allow yourself to become a little more centered with each breath
- o Continue to breathe through your nose until you feel relaxed and centered in your body
- o Now think of yourself
- o Exhale and repeat I LOVE MYSELF
- o Inhale and repeat I am free from suffering
- o Inhale and repeat I am experiencing the highest form of happiness

- Inhale and repeat I am the embodiment of love

Repeat the above twice

- Breathe through your nose a few times
- Allow your body and mind to soften
- Feel your sit bones and relax even further
- Maybe there's a little more space between your ears and shoulders
- Continue to breathe through your nose
- Allow yourself to become a little more centered with each breath
- Continue to breathe through your nose until you feel relaxed and centered in your body
- Gently come back to the present moment

Backsliding Strategies

- When challenging moments occur and your mood is down, flip the switch through self-care
- Utilize the smiling meditation to enhance your mood in any moment
- Share kindness and self-compassion to yourself to strengthen your mindset of joyful and positive

CHAPTER 6: MINDFUL EXISTENCE
Be curious and playful in the process

Create your own Persona:

- First to see your patterns, what persona have you been living into
- Where you can improve your responses
- Develop and create yourself as you wish to be
- Add self-love through the kindness meditation
- Create who you want to be in every given moment, no matter what your past decisions have been

Triggers:

- Acknowledge your external triggers and add compassion to yourself internally so you may have more fruitful relationships with your colleagues.
- Other people have ways of dealing with heir stress that may not jive with you or your true nature

4 takeaways are

- Acknowledge the response you've had
- Add compassion internally to yourself
- Reframe the trigger externally, adding compassion to the people you're interacting with

- o   Move on, creating a positive and joyful persona I wished to embrace

CHAPTER 7: FIND LIKE-MINDED PEOPLE
Build a community

Surround yourself with like-minded people
- o   Acknowledge yourself as a joyful positive person and find other like-minded people
- o   Build a community filled with constructive & meaningful relationships

Use power words for internal & external dialog Mindfully
- o   Remove negative connotations from your internal and external language
- o   Become mindful of the language you use in your mind and that you use when speaking

Replace words with negative connotations, with positive ones
- o   This is Difficult -> This is Challenging
- o   I need x -> I want x
- o   I will -> wouldn't it be nice
- o   I'm getting in shape -> I'm staying in shape

- I fear an outcome -> I have a plan to navigate the outcome I fear

- Find the root cause of negative internal dialog & use Chapter 1's exercise to reframe it
- Chapter 1's excerpt is plausible for internal and external dialog patterns and alleviating root causes:

Own your decision to feel a certain way & flip the switch to a joyful existence:
- Compassionately acknowledge you've embraced an emotion or thought process
- Fill your personal space with joyful bodily expressions like smiling and positive thoughts.
- Find the root cause or belief of why I'm embracing sadness and wallowing
- Rethink its rationality
- Reframe the situation that caused your decision to feel a certain way, make it positive
- And moved on with the emotion you choose to fill your head space

Infuse celebrating and Laughter in your life
- It's the little things that bring joy, celebrate them at every opportunity

- Practice being grateful for these moments, events, friends and loved ones
- Laugh more often & use the smile meditation to get your mindset joyful
- Teach others that it's normal to be joyful when you meet at work or in your personal life
- Smile at work, remove the stern 'all business' face mask
- Say hello to colleagues
- Be Mindfully aware of others: Walk down the hallway mindfully, be aware of who is around and say hello to them
- Create light-hearted dialog and create friendly relationships before meetings and at the end of the workday
- Detach from any expectations that your joyful attitude will yield a result with colleagues and you'll see more results

Stay Present: Don't look back or be embarrassed by your old habits, stay present in the moment with who you are today.

Thank you for your time and attention. Have a blessed day & best wishes to you.

Michelle Jeffalone

46970382R00062

Made in the USA
Middletown, DE
13 August 2017